HEALING

---

the wounded child

WITHIN

Heal Your Wounds, Change Your Life

HEALING

the wounded child

WITHIN

Heal Your Wounds, Change Your Life

RICKY ROBERTS III

IP INDEPENDENTLY PUBLISHED

Cover Design: Keith Burnson
Editor: Sarah Dinetz
Bio Photo: Joey Clay ©
Cover Photo: Ryan Loughlin

Published in the United States of America
1. Self-Help / Inner Child
2. Self-Help / Personal Transformation
18.01.24

Table of Contents

PREFACE

There was a time when I allowed the wounds from my childhood to control my life. Watching as my father's struggle with drug and alcohol abuse divided our family made me angry. Him leaving when I was twelve, and me not seeing or talking to him, with the exception of a few times, until I was twenty-two, made me feel abandoned and that I wasn't worthy of being loved. Seeing my mother endure abuse, physically, emotionally, and mentally, by multiple men, including my father, made me feel useless. Being abused the same way as a child made me not trust anyone. We were evicted from multiple homes, went without electricity and water at different times, and relied on hand-me-downs for school clothes, which made me feel ashamed about myself. I was hurting and had no clue how to address the pain I carried. In fact, I worked hard to hide it from others and was too embarrassed to get help. I fought a lot as a youth. In some ways, I wanted to die, and sometimes wished that I would. I lived recklessly and put myself in harm's way far too often.

My life changed when I was stabbed nine times during a street fight at the age of seventeen. It took me lying in the hospital bed covered in blood, with open wounds all over my body and face, to realize that it wasn't ever that I really wanted to die; I just didn't know how to live. I spent the next week in the hospital thinking about how much I was allowing the things I witnessed and experienced as a child to control who I was, how I thought and felt about myself, and how I treated others. I didn't know what exactly I would do to change my life, but I knew I had to do something. It was then that I started the long journey of healing the pain that clouded my ability to find joy in my life.

Over the years, I have had to remember things I hoped to forget, in order to heal the pain that I suppressed for so long. I have had to be honest with myself in times when it felt way easier to keep denying the truth of my wounds and doing what I could to forget them.

As I began to connect my patterns of failed relationships, negative views of myself, and unhealthy thoughts to their root causes, I noticed how much the wounds of my childhood played a part in them.

It has been quite the journey of my own healing. Some of it has been painful to look at, but there has never been a time after addressing these issues when I didn't feel relief.

I still have unresolved wounds from my past, and healing them is an ongoing process, but now that I approach them for what they are, the wounded child within, they have become much easier to work through.

The child that was wounded in the past is a part of who we are in the present. We can't deny this. The way in which we see the world, in many aspects, is through its eyes. It is important to honor it and do our best to make it better.

Can we love the wounded child within unconditionally? Can—and should—we ease its pain? Can we show it that being happy and helping others is much better than the pain we've been holding onto?

Unfortunately, we all carry pain from our past. It is

not an easy thing to accept or admit. However, when you give your wounds the time, thought, and attention they need in order to be healed, the load you carry will lighten and your life will change.

By change, I don't exactly mean a clouds-parting-in-the-sky, aha-type moment. I mean change on a fundamental level. This book is not just about making you feel good as you read it; it is a tool that will help you facilitate your own work. Some parts of it may not make you feel good at all, because of the thoughts, likely suppressed, it will bring up. Unfortunately, sometimes it takes facing the pain in order to keep rising above it. The reward will not come just from acknowledging the wounds from your past, but also from choosing to do the work that will help you heal them.

I recommend you getting a pen, so that you can engage with the reflection questions and activities at the end of each section. Of course, if you are someone who likes to pass your books on or lend them to others, you may want to get a notebook or journal to write in. You may opt to read the questions without writing down your responses. However, I believe that, if you write down your answers and spend time reflecting on them, it will add to your experience with this book and potentially contribute to the well-being of your life on many levels.

Whether or not you choose to spend extra time on the questions and activities, take your time. Allow it to bring to light things from your past that may be holding you back in the present, things that may limit your greatest potential in the future.

We have all been hurt, lied to, disrespected, mistreated, or put down at some point in our lives. Some of us have felt any combination—or all—of those things, some in much more dramatic ways than others. No matter what the extent is, or was, it compromised our ability to see the greatness in who we are, to love without fear, to be vulnerable, and to trust others enough to get close to them.

The pure essence of our untainted spirit becomes wounded, and becomes more wounded every time we experience anything other than the love, support, and encouragement we deserve.

We come into this world knowing peace, love, and

innocence, and are essentially free from any knowledge of hurt. Our life experience begins with seeing the world with a peaceful and open heart. From there, everything else is learned. Over time, generation after generation, culture after culture, people continue to operate from the wounds they developed as a child. The wounded child becomes the ruler of our world and our own individual reality. Cycles of fear, abuse, neglect, violence, and poverty are repeated.

By learning to understand the root from which our own pain comes, and how to heal it, we will not only become better versions of ourselves, but we will create a better world for us all.

IDENTIFY THE WOUNDS

Often times, when we think of a wounded child, we think of someone who grew up in an abusive home, one who witnessed abuse and/or experienced it in one capacity or another. We think of the one that ends up in prison—or dead—and the troubled kid that walks into a school, shoots people, and kills his or herself. Maybe we think of the one who takes their own life because of how wounded they are from being bullied. In other words, we think of the extremes.

Those are obvious, and all too common, examples of children who are wounded inside. They are so hurt that they are hurting others and/or themselves. They didn't come into this world with the idea of committing violent crimes, being in prison, or feeling so much pain inside that they commit suicide. None of us do. They came in, like we all do, wanting to feel safe and loved. Somewhere along the way, they became wounded. The wounds became worse, and, at some point, manifested themselves through horrific choices.

Those are some of the extremes.

Now, what about the child who doesn't fall that far into the pain and negativity of their wounds? The one who may not necessarily seem wounded on the surface, but is? These are the ones dealing with being let down in some way or another. Maybe their parents or guardians are getting divorced, or their trust has been broken on some level, or they have pain caused by a loved one. What about the ones with the wounds that almost everyone can relate to, regardless of how extreme or not?

No matter what the severity is, the wounds from our childhood carry forward into our adult life. Feelings of anxiety, anger, bitterness, lack of self-worth, issues with trust, and/or a sense of abandonment may be connected to the wounds of the innocent child that only knew love, until it was shown something different.

The foundation of our existence is built on the

experiences we have. One after another, they form the perception of our reality.

The first several years of our life happen with us having virtually no control. The people trusted with our care have a huge impact on our development. So many factors contribute to our sense of the world: the way people treat us, what we experience, the kind of environment we grow up in, the love we get (or don't), the words we hear others speak to us, about us, and/or around us, and even the movies we see and songs we listen to.

As we seek to understand who we are, build relationships, and decipher our emotions, we unknowingly go back to the understanding we gained of what the world is. The wounded child within surfaces.

Though fears, anxiety, low self-esteem, trust issues, insecurities, and anger are often rooted in what we learned as a child, this is in no way to establish a misplacement of blame on our issues, nor is it to say that anything—or everything—we feel as an adult is not real and only represents our childhood. The intent is to identify the parts of who we are that distract us from our highest and best good, which, in many cases, is related to the wounded child within.

Physical, emotional, and psychological forms of abuse were a common and regular part of the environment in which I grew up in. I had more experiences with my trust being broken than I did with having it built up.

There are some great memories I do have with both of my parents, as well as some of my relatives. One of my favorite memories as a child is of me walking in on my mom and dad wrapping presents on Christmas Eve. I will never forget them looking up at me surprised, and asking if I wanted to help. We stayed awake most of the night listening to Christmas music, eating "Santa's" cookies that we left out for him, and wrapping my brothers and sisters presents. My mom and dad were smiling and laughing all night. They seemed genuinely happy and I couldn't have been any happier, as a child, than what I was in that moment.

Unfortunately, the times that were not as good were much more frequent, which made for me not believing in the good times when they did happen. They actually felt uncomfortable to me. As much as I wanted to be comfortable when things seemed to be going well, I knew deep down that they usually did not last. The fights and the blood and the raised voices were what I was most familiar with. My childhood, for the most part, was a perpetual cycle of dysfunction, abuse, neglect, and violence. It was hard to feel safe because I never knew when things would erupt.

I do not blame anyone for things that happened, or didn't happen, throughout my childhood. I hold no ill will toward my parents or family members. In fact, I appreciate the many ways they did try to do what was right, within the capacity of their abilities, while dealing with their own pain and confusion.

The truth is that, as much as I like to think I would have made better choices than my parents and others who had a negative impact on my life, I can't say for sure that I would have. What I do know for sure, however, is that the choices that were made by others had such a negative impact on my well-being that I have spent the better part of my life undoing the damage that was done.

Once I was able to identify my issues and where they came from, I was able to do a better job of managing them which, in return, minimizes the negative impact they have on my life.

Think about the different negative patterns and cycles that may be playing out in your life. Identify what they are, where they come from, and how much they affect you. These may be good to write down. I personally like to write things down, pen to paper, and find it to be more powerful and effective when I do. Once you identify and assess the negative patterns, think intently about the things, experiences, and types of people that trigger them, and how they play out in your life. How are they holding you back? What does your life look like if those negative patterns no longer were a part of it?

If we don't identify the problems that exist, as well as where they are coming from, we will never have the awareness and know how to fix them. As we identify the wounds that may be holding us back, we become even freer to live life to our fullest potential.

Reflect and Engage

When was the first time you were hurt by someone you cared about?

_____

_____

_____

_____

_____

_____

_____

_____

_____

_____

_____

_____

How did it make you feel in that moment?

_____

_____

_____

_____

_____

_____

Detail a situation in which you were made fun of or put down by someone you looked up to.

_____

_____

_____

_____

_____

_____

_____

_____

_____

_____

_____

How often in your childhood were you encouraged, supported, and made to feel special? Was this as much as you think you should have been?

_____

_____

_____

_____

_____

_____

_____

_____

_____

_____

_____

_____

_____

_____

_____

_____

_____

_____

_____

_____

Looking back on times you were hurt, let down, or told you weren't good enough, how do you believe those experiences impacted the way you see, think, and feel about yourself now?

_____

_____

_____

_____

_____

_____

_____

_____

_____

_____

_____

_____

_____

_____

_____

_____

_____

_____

_____

Before we move on, I'd like to share a powerful exercise that really helped me identify wounds that I needed to address.

As I began to take my growth and healing seriously, I knew there were a lot of painful memories that I'd suppressed, ignored, and/or forgotten that I needed to address.

I would lie in bed, close my eyes, and start reflecting on painful memories, allowing myself to dwell on them. It's important to note that I only allowed myself to dwell in these sessions, not in my daily life. I would start with the first thing I could remember as a child and let my memory flow from there, with the intent of finding the ones that brought me pain.

As memories that brought feelings of sadness, anger, and/or pain came up, I would not avoid them. Instead, I would stay with them, thinking about details, sounds, and feelings. I would stare my pain in the face, one memory at a time. I stayed present with the pain, allowing myself to really feel it. Then, I would imagine that hurt, afraid, and lonely child that was once me, and is still a part of me, feeling loved.

I kept with the memory as long as I could, to soften the hardness around it. I went on to the next painful memory and would go on until I felt done for the night. My capacity was different each night, depending on how much emotion came up with the memory. There were some nights when I could hardly stop the tears. On others, I got angry, and, for some, I felt numb.

I did this night after night for several months. Each night, I would start as far back as I could remember. I looked for painful memories to give them love. Over time, the memories felt less and less painful each time they came up. Some of them were not easy to face, at first, but eventually got easier as I gave them love and attention.

Now, after doing this on a regular basis, there are no memories that I feel uncomfortable facing. I have recounted them enough to feel at ease if they are triggered, or even if they come up randomly.

I have always been a dive-into-the-deep-end sort of person. Having said that, I am not suggesting you do this exercise every night like I chose to, especially when you are just getting started. It is up to you to decide how often you want to pursue this. You know what works best for you. Please respect that.

A lot of pain will surface during this exercise. There will be things that may come up that you had no real conscious memory of, as there were for me. It can be intense. There is no shame in whatever you may find. None of this is your fault, and you will feel so much better in the long run as you address these wounds.

There is no hurry with this work. Take your time. Maybe you feel like reflecting on one painful memory a week is good for you, or maybe you prefer more frequently. The choice is yours. The goal of the exercise is to identify wounds from your past and give them love. You may be surprised how much healing comes simply from giving them attention.

Get yourself comfortable. Close your eyes. Let the pain come up. Give it love. Repeat.

Forgiveness

Forgiveness is an intricate part of healing the wounded child within. Before any true healing can sustain, we must forgive the people, things, and situations that hurt us. We must also forgive ourselves.

Forgive those who have hurt you, and find resolve in the times you felt abandoned, let down, and like you were not enough. Also, most importantly, forgive yourself. Not every person or situation will be easy to forgive. The key is to have the courage and willingness to start at all.

I carried a lot of resentment toward my mother and father for a long time. I blamed them for the internal struggles I faced as an adult, as a result of choices they made when I was a child. I knew that, if I didn't forgive them, the anger I felt toward them would keep holding me back.

The best place to start will be different for everyone. One good trick I've found, however, is writing a letter to someone you want to forgive, even if that person is you. You certainly don't have to give it to them, but, if you feel inspired to, please do. The act of writing the letter alone can be quite healing. I have used this practice several times to write people who have hurt me, or people who I've hurt.

When I first started seeing the need to work on forgiveness in my life, I wrote a letter to my father and mother addressing the pain I felt as a child because of different choices they made. The letter gave the wounded child within me a chance to communicate what it felt like to be him at the time and me the opportunity, as an adult, to acknowledge those feelings. It was profoundly healing and helped me become vulnerable to the wounds that held me back for so long. More importantly, it gave the wounded child within me a voice, which was the start of my ability to forgive my parents.

Sharing the letter is difficult, but it has been a

crucial part of the healing process for me. I'm hoping it will serve the same purpose for you.

Dear Mom and Dad,

Who are you and where did you come from? My mind has been clouded by visions that are not my own, distracted from dreams I had for myself. Who are you and where did you come from? I am that little boy that was thrown out from his own existence. Hurt so bad he left his innocence at the place where you first called him useless, MOM, and at the place where he first saw you drunk, DAD!

Where did the kid go? I'm looking for you. I know you are in there, but I don't know how far you have slipped away into the dark hole of silence that you hide in. Do you remember where you were and where you were lost? What is the last thing you remember?

Here I am! I'm over here. Does anyone see me? I'm trying to show my face, but no one wants to listen. The second I begin to pop up, you hurt me, so I crawl back into my safe place. I don't want you to know my pain, but this time I slip further away. Mom and Dad, do you know that every time you hit me, or call me names, it puts another scar on my already hardened heart?

I act crazy at school, I fight, I yell, I act like I don't care, I feel like I want to die, but deep down all that I really want is love. Do you even know who I am? Do you know that I have a child inside of me who wants to play, but he can't because he is afraid to come out and face the pain? Instead what you see is an angry child who looks for a reason to hide just so he doesn't have to be here anymore.

Mom and Dad, please look at me! I am sitting here in this house full of people, but I still feel alone. If you don't know by now, I will tell you: the innocence in me is slipping away.

I'm eight now. You keep leaving me alone with my older cousins to babysit me. Did you know that, when you left, part of my innocence went with you every time? Did you not hear me when I told you I didn't like being with them, or that I was afraid? Did you ever hear anything I said to you? Did you notice the bruises across my body, or the bite marks on my back? Maybe you can hear me now. They made me fight and would not let me stop, even when I was begging them to just leave me alone. I would lie there as they beat me. If I didn't fight back, they would hurt me worse. I didn't want to fight my family, but they made me.

This is my house. I am not safe here. Why do you leave me, when I ask you not to? I'm only a kid.

Your once innocent child is leaving to a further place, now. There is a new child born. This one wants to fight back. This one gets angry. He wants to hurt people. He wants others to feel his pain because you never took the time to. Neither one of you care. I get it now; I truly am alone in a house full of people.

I just asked you if you got one without onions for me! I'm sorry I upset you, Dad. Did you ever question what I felt when you threw the whole bag of food at me because I asked a question? Mom, did you know how bad it hurt me when you blamed me for him being angry?

I'm ten now. I don't remember what it is to be a kid anymore. The only thing I want to do now is run the streets. I don't want to be near either one of you. I will leave when I wake up and do my best to stay gone as long as I can. As much as I try to stay away, I still just want to be noticed. Mom, Dad, can I at least have a hug when I leave, or a kiss when I go to bed? Oh wait, I'm sorry. Maybe that is just the kid in me crying for attention. You're right. I don't need affection from you. I'm okay in this house full of people feeling like I am alone.

No, not again. Don't wake me up to see this. Mom, do you really think I want to see my father hitting you? I suppose you thought it would make him stop, but it hurt me to know I couldn't stop him. Dad, stop, I'm here! I'm your little boy. Am I not enough to make you stop? It's okay. I'm a man now; I can take it. You're both here, but I still feel alone. I'm afraid.

Dad, it's my birthday. Can you put down the crack pipe just for one day? Did you see the sadness in my eyes when I walked in on you smoking crack on my birthday? I'm sorry that I cried. I know I'm not a child anymore, and "big kids are not suppose to cry." I'll try better next time; just don't be mad at me.

Mom and Dad, I'm eleven now. The only feeling that I have is anger. I know the little boy is in there but I feel nothing. I am calling for him, but he doesn't respond. I see now, the child is gone. My innocence is no more. Now it is up to me. I can no longer turn to you for what I need. I realize that you are not the ones who will give me the love I am asking for. Mom, you keep telling me that I will be just like him. Dad, you are never around to say anything. Is it me? Did I do something wrong?

Wait…. wait…. don't go. Daddy! Daddy! Come back! I see the child running behind you. He won't stop chasing you! He has left me for good to be with you.

Mom, please say anything. Will I see him again? Where is he going? Can you please just hug me, anything, something?

I hurt so badly. I just want to be loved.
Your little boy,
Ricky

When writing my own letter, I surprised myself with some of the stuff I wrote. Share your emotions, open and honestly. It will liberate you and the wounded child within. Let your inner child have his or her chance to speak truth to the ones that hurt them.

Keep in mind that, just because you forgive someone, this does not mean you forget, or agree with, what they did. The act of forgiveness is to free and heal yourself, not the people that hurt you. When you forgive them, it will help heal the wounds they caused.

Part of the pain you still carry is because of the bitterness you hold in your heart toward people that hurt you. An important thing to remember is that it's not your fault. I have found that, in the process of forgiveness, we tend to find ways to justify the pain others caused, or put the blame on ourselves. Don't do it. It doesn't help.

If there is something you did wrong or something that caused pain to yourself or others, I want to remind you that it's okay. Nobody is perfect. The best thing you can do is hold yourself accountable. Acknowledge that you could have made, and can make, different choices. Learn and grow from your mistakes, commit to doing better, and let it go. Holding onto resentment and bitterness toward yourself is just as bad as, if not worse than, holding onto resentment toward someone else.

Wherever or however you can start forgiving people who have hurt you, do it. If you don't forgive, the pain will not go away. The sad reality is that it will slowly eat away at the well-being of your heart, and you certainly don't deserve that.

Reflect and Engage

Name the three (or more) people who caused the most pain in your life when you were a child. The goal here is to focus on the wounds that have been stored away in the past.

_____

_____

_____

_____

_____

_____

_____

_____

_____

_____

Think about those people, one by one, and reflect on your feelings about them. What do you feel when you think about them?

_____

_____

_____

_____

_____

_____

_____

_____

_____

_____

_____

_____

_____

_____

_____

_____

_____

_____

_____

What pain did they cause you?

_____

_____

_____

_____

_____

_____

_____

_____

_____

_____

_____

_____

_____

_____

_____

_____

_____

_____

_____

_____

How did it, and still does it, impact your life?

_____

_____

_____

_____

_____

_____

_____

_____

_____

_____

_____

_____

_____

_____

_____

_____

_____

_____

_____

_____

_____

Take your time with this. Let whatever emotions come up for you have their time and place. It's a part of the healing process.

After you've spent some time reflecting on the questions above and have a good sense of your feelings about the people you listed, start with writing a letter to at least one of them. Eventually, if you feel inspired to, writing a letter to all three (or more, if you listed additional people) will be liberating. I highly recommend it.

I know this book can be intense, so feel free to take a break if you're feeling overwhelmed. Lay down. Put some relaxing music on. Meditate. Pray. Journal. Paint. Or, simply just sit there. Let any of the emotions that may have surfaced for you have the time to settle. Lean into the beauty of who you are, and the peace you feel in your heart by choosing to forgive yourself and others.

Keep showing up!

Seeing The Wounded Child Within

To fully understand the wounds within us and how they hold us back, we need to see them for what they are and appreciate the roles they play in our life. When we have negative reactions, or act out of character towards others, it's important to recognize the part that our wounded child may play in it. He or she is a real part of who we are and deserves to be respected as such.

Side note: It is also important to point out that it is not just the wounded child we see play out in our life. We must also appreciate the happy, creative, inspired, and adventurous child, just the same. This is the part of our inner child that we can all stand to nurture and allow to become a driving force in our life.

Your inner child is worthy of being seen.

When we react to certain situations or circumstances with fear, anger, insecurities, doubt, and/or lack of trust, more times than not, the behavior is rooted in unresolved wounds from childhood. We respond to the situation from a time and place where we were first hurt, let down, mistreated, abandoned, or abused, as well as the times that followed. Unfortunately, those same feelings are reinforced multiple times throughout life.

Our psyche doesn't always differentiate between the times when the emotions were first experienced and the cause in the present moment. In this case, although the current experience may be painful, and certainly triggered a spark in emotions, the emotional and physical responses are also coming from a much deeper place, the part of your subconscious that is perceiving and understanding the world from past experiences.

Often times, when certain emotions play out, you are seeing yourself in the present, and also as part of the pain of a wounded child. This is not to discount the pain we feel in the present or suggest that it is not real. Pain is real at anytime you feel it. There is simply more to it.

Let's say you are in love with someone. You've found a great significant other, and you see them as your world. They are the person that you have so patiently been waiting for. In your mind, this is it. You are convinced you want to spend your life with them. Everything is going amazingly well!

Things change. You're fighting a lot. The extent of your pain feels unbearable. You can't sleep or eat, and you feel completely abandoned. The mix of emotions that you feel is very real. However, on that same note, there is a part of the experience—the root cause to most of the pain you feel—that is triggering something much deeper.

Yes, some of the emotions you feel are certainly coming from the situation itself. However, they are also coming from the unhealed and unresolved wounds from things that happened to you as a child. This situation can vary from person to person. Maybe your significant other yells in traffic, which is completely normal amongst some drivers, but it brings you back to your father yelling at you all the time. Perhaps you were made to feel inferior your whole life, so your partner's bragging about everything has taken its toll on you.

There are many other examples that may relate to your life. Chances are, there is something deeper there, still in the process of being resolved, otherwise it would not have impacted you so immensely. When something like a fight in a relationship or break-up occurs, we not only face the pain of that experience, but we also deal with past hurt that surfaces because of it. We begin to simultaneously bear the burden of the two hurt identities. It's like dealing with being two hurt people at the same time. When you really peel back the layers, the main source of your pain tends to be coming from your wounded child.

Does this mean what happened hasn't impacted you? No. Does this mean that you are too sensitive and you will never thrive in relationships? No. It means the deeper pain you feel is coming from a part of you that has not been healed. Over time, you have become okay with the deep-rooted pain and continue to suppress it, but the burdens you carry because of it haven't gone away. The burdens will remain until you address them, which makes the work you are doing now that much more important.

When we see the wounded child aspect of who we

are, and honor it as a part of us, we can better learn how to address and heal it.

Once you become aware of the triggers as they occur, you're able to better differentiate between the pain you are feeling in the moment and the pain coming up from your past.

When your wounds are triggered and they seem to get the best of you, take your emotions out of the situation. This can seem tricky, but it makes a world of difference. Take ownership of any areas you fell short and can improve. Look at it objectively. Are you taking it personally? Should you be nearly as upset, or bothered by it, as you are? Where is the pain really coming from? What exactly are you feeling? When was the last time you felt this way, and what caused it?

Keep talking yourself through it until your emotions subside and you are able to experience the situation with more ease.

Reflect and Engage

Name an experience that felt more painful than you may have expected, given the circumstances.

_____

_____

_____

_____

_____

_____

_____

_____

_____

_____

_____

Can you make a connection between that particular experience and an underlying issue stemming from your childhood? Explain.

_____

_____

_____

_____

_____

_____

_____

_____

_____

_____

_____

_____

_____

_____

_____

_____

_____

_____

_____

Besides dealing with a break-up (or something similar in nature), what are different events in your life during which the wounded child within has surfaced?

_____

_____

_____

_____

_____

_____

_____

_____

_____

_____

_____

_____

_____

_____

_____

_____

_____

_____

_____

_____

Before you read on, please take a few minutes to acknowledge how much you have already worked through to be who you are today, and commend yourself for the work you're choosing to do now in order to facilitate your greatest enjoyment in life.

You are doing amazing!

LEARNING MORE ABOUT THE CHILD WITHIN

In order to no longer be a victim of my past wounds, I had to address them. I could not allow what I endured as a child—the yelling, witnessing violence, being hit with wooden spoons—cause me to spend my life making excuses for being hypersensitive and hurtful toward others and myself as an adult. Eventually, I started to see that these things I wanted to heal and change were not just about letting go of the past, but that they also play out in the present.

There are a variety of situations that have triggered the wounded child within, and, whenever they happened, I felt the pain of that child in the present.

Some of the many unpredictable and somewhat random things that trigger my inner child are holiday functions, loud noises, large crowds, movies that show things that relate to me as a kid, driving by certain restaurants or parks I went to as a young person, getting a reminder letter to pay a bill, and even the smell of certain foods that remind me of my childhood.

Sometimes I anticipate that specific situations will trigger my wounds, but, other times, it happens by complete surprise. I was helping a good friend remodel the bathroom at his house, and, as we were building the frame for the window, we ran into a few complications. Out of frustration, he started yelling and slamming things. It was not overly aggressive, nor was he directing any of it at me, but I still got uncomfortably anxious. I suddenly felt like a scared child getting yelled at, so I walked outside to let my friend work through his frustration. I think it is safe to assume that none of us really like being around yelling or things being thrown, but what I felt in the moment was much more intense than me not liking it. The situation triggered feelings of anxiety and fear from past wounds. The experience really surprised me, especially since I feel so safe around this person. I knew, as an adult, that this was not a hostile or hurtful situation, but the wounded child within me didn't know the difference.

Acknowledge your inner child as an actual person, not just a memory. It may sound strange, but it really helps. See it as an identity that exists within you, that sometimes lives out its need for healing through you as an adult. Sure, it has matured, grown, and let things go... but it has not gone away. There are experiences you have as an adult that are more emotionally driven by your wounded child than your current self. This is when the wounded child takes over.

My mother lied to me a lot when I was growing up. Whether it was the amount of money my dad was suppose to send us, what the truth was about a man she was dating, or a terminal illness she claimed to have, she told lies often. There was always a part of me that wanted to believe her, no matter how many times she'd lied to me before. She would generally keep the stories going on for months, just long enough to make me think that maybe she was telling the truth this time. The disappointment and sad reality took its toll on me. Every time I tried to trust again, the trust was broken. I felt alone and began to not trust anyone.

It took me a long time to be able to trust people

again. As close as I seemed to let others get, I kept them at a distance, always waiting for the little trust I did build with them to be compromised. I wanted to trust them, but, anytime I felt vulnerable to being hurt, I quickly became the wounded child who could not trust anyone. The walls went up. I projected the broken trust I'd developed as a child onto the people I tried to have relationships with as an adult. Whether they were people I dated, or close friends, I would anticipate the ways they would hurt me. This was not good, to say the least. I believed that I couldn't trust anyone, but really it was the wounded child within that felt that way. It was not me in the present.

In most cases, I didn't have any evidence or reason not to trust people. The deeper I looked at it, the more I saw it was actually two different identities interacting with trying to be vulnerable, simultaneously. On one hand, I would approach situations as an intelligent adult, trying to let people in. On the other hand, a wounded child afraid of being hurt would look for every reason not to.

When we are able to look at our emotional state with an awareness of a wounded child that may be participating consciously or subconsciously, we can see more clearly how to manage it. When your wounded child surfaces, stop, do not respond, observe the situation, and use it as an opportunity to learn and grow. Name it for what it is. *I know these feelings of pain are from my past. I am safe and have no need to be afraid. No one is trying to hurt me here. I honor what is happening right now and will handle it from here. My wounds will not control my life.* Take deep breaths while you work through it, and, if necessary and possible, remove yourself from the environment. After you work through your emotions and pacify the needs of your inner child, look for things about the situation that are positive. It never hurts to create positive associations around things that take us back to a bad place. Take note of what the triggers were and reflect on why they so greatly impacted you. If you feel comfortable doing so, let the person know what they did that upset you. This is not an overnight process. It is a lifelong journey. The beautiful thing is that you are willing to put the work in, and it will make all the difference.

Reflect and Engage

Is it easy for you to trust people?

If so, was it always that way? Did you have a loving and supportive family that fostered trust, or is it something that you had to work on?

If not, why do you think it is hard for you to trust people?

_____

_____

_____

_____

_____

_____

_____

_____

_____

_____

_____

_____

_____

_____

_____

_____

_____

_____

_____

_____

_____

_____

_____

_____

_____

_____

_____

_____

_____

_____

_____

What is at least one issue you have (an insecurity, jealousy, lack of self-worth, need to control everything, fear of success, etc.) that you think comes from your childhood?

How does it play out in your life?

_____

_____

_____

_____

_____

_____

_____

_____

_____

_____

_____

_____

_____

_____

_____

_____

_____

Share an experience when you feel like the wounded child within took control, when it was as if you were reacting from its pain and not your aware and mature self as an adult.

_____

_____

_____

_____

_____

_____

_____

_____

_____

_____

_____

_____

_____

_____

_____

_____

_____

_____

Don't Blame the Child

Because we have learned to identify and explore more about our wounded child, this does not mean we should ever blame him or her for our behavior. We have to be accountable for how we handle ourselves, wounded child or not. It is not anyone else's duty or obligation; it is ours. We cannot simply say, "Oh, that's my wounded child acting out. It's not my fault." Although it is very helpful to identify and understand the wounded child within, it is equally as important to acknowledge our responsibility to manage it, as adults.

Ultimately, we are the only ones responsible for our own behavior. If you witnessed your parents hitting each other, and you hit your spouse, does it make it okay?

Absolutely not! Just because it may be what is familiar to you, that does not make it okay, ever. We have to be accountable for who we are and the choices we make. The truth is, sometimes it is easier to just blame our past. I get it. I played the blame game for a long time, justifying my issues with my childhood experiences, especially in my relationships. As much work as I thought I was doing to heal myself, I still defaulted to blaming the past instead of being accountable for how I could fix the things that held me back.

The moment something happens in your life that you start to blame your wounded child for-- stop. Take ownership, and ask how you can defuse the situation and help make it better. What is your role in the issues that cause problems, and what can you do change them?

As the wounded child presents itself in the times of distress, it is our duty to redirect, discipline, and validate him or her.

When you feel your wounded child about to start acting out, you are responsible for redirecting them before they get too far out of line. Do something in the moment that will calm them. Tell him or her things that will make them feel better, encouraged, loved, supported, and seen. By working to heal your wounds instead of making excuses and placing blame, there is a smaller chance that any of it will control your life.

I appreciate that it can be frustrating to deal with some of the issues that stem from your childhood. Sometimes it may even seem unfair, as other people likely didn't experience what you did, or don't deal with the same issues you do. It's okay to feel the way you do. An important thing to remember is that you can't change any of it now. All you can do is change how you react to it. It is a part of you.

Reflect and Engage

Have you ever acted poorly as an adult and blamed it on your childhood? Explain.

_____

_____

_____

_____

_____

_____

_____

_____

_____

_____

_____

What aspects of your life do you see the wounded child within taking control of?

_____

_____

_____

_____

_____

_____

_____

_____

_____

_____

_____

_____

_____

_____

_____

_____

_____

_____

_____

_____

When the wounded child within gets out of line, what can you do to change it?

_____

_____

_____

_____

_____

_____

_____

_____

_____

_____

_____

_____

_____

_____

_____

_____

_____

_____

_____

_____

What are strategies you can use to maintain control and clarity when your wounds are triggered?

_____

_____

_____

_____

_____

_____

_____

_____

_____

_____

_____

_____

_____

_____

_____

_____

_____

_____

Here is an exercise that may feel good for you to do during this process. Think of an experience you had as a child that hurt you. Think about how you felt and what you needed to hear—but never did—back then.

On a piece of paper, write a letter to that child, the you who existed then. I know it may sound a bit weird, but it'll be worth it. Tell him or her that they will be okay. Better yet, tell them everything that you only wish you'd heard in that moment.

I suggest you spend a little extra time with this and the feelings that may come up. Relax, journal, and reflect. Above all, applaud yourself for having such courage to work through these issues. I know it's not easy, but it is so freeing when you do.

Keep up the great work!

Your Beliefs About Money & Abundance

In addition to our interactions and relationships being impacted by the experiences we had as a child, our beliefs about money are also impacted.

I grew up poor. There was mostly fear, stress, anger, and pain around the topic of money. It wasn't uncommon, at some points in time, for the water or electricity to be turned off due to bills not being paid. What we ate was often determined by the boxes of food local churches would give us.

There was a period of time in high school that my morning shower was in my backyard using a gallon of water I got from the convenient store nearby. I would stand outside in shorts, pour water over my head, rub a little soap on me, and pour more water on myself to rinse off. I felt embarrassed and ashamed. I certainly didn't speak about it with any of my friends or teachers. For the most part, I pretended like everything was okay. Needless to say, luxuries beyond basic necessities were never a good topic of discussion for most of my childhood.

I went through childhood trying to figure out how to get my own money to buy things like school clothes, skateboards, and food. Shortly after graduating high school, I felt inspired to take what I'd learned from my own struggles to help youth. I studied child development at a junior college, with the intention of pursuing a psychology or counseling track while working as a group leader for a child care agency. I was great at what I did and felt really good about the path I was on at the time.

In the meantime, on the way to the elementary school I was working at, I got into an accident and totaled my first car. While I was in the process of finding a new one, a friend told me about a dependable used car dealership that I should check out. I listened to his advice and ended up buying a car from them.

The owner and I got along really well from the start. There was something about him that I felt drawn to. I looked up to him in a lot of ways and found myself stopping by the dealership randomly just to chat with him. Eventually, he offered me a part-time job, which I took. Several months later, he asked if I would work for him full-time, offering me a salary quite impressive at that stage in my life. My first response was, "No, thank you. I love working with kids and I don't want to leave my job working with them." Over time, however, I was pulled to what I thought was the lifestyle and freedom money would bring me. I took him up on the opportunity.

After having a little glimpse into what it looked like to have money and break free from the cycle of poverty, I became very motivated to reach financial success. It felt good to have the means to buy nice things for the first time in my life. Over the course of ten years, I moved up in positions and eventually bought the business, making monthly installments to purchase the name, inventory, and a small ownership percentage of the property.

Having extra money gave me a false sense of freedom and allowed me to experience the temporary satisfaction of "nice" things, fancy cars, and fine dining. But it did not fulfill me.

It wasn't long after we signed the agreement and I was fully committed to around one million dollars, through various contracts, that I got the strong sense that it was time for me to leave. I'd achieved something that I thought would feel so good—but it didn't. Honestly, I was quite surprised by the feelings that I had. Eventually, after a few discussions with the original owner, the contracts between us were dissolved, and I was able to walk away. I lost quite a bit of money—and still owed him more when I left, which I paid back over time—but I was very thankful to be able to leave.

I enjoyed my time in the car business and learned a lot. Though I am so grateful that I got out when I did, I know I was meant to be there for those ten years. So much of what I learned in my time there has helped me in countless ways.

Although I did well financially there, and appreciated the people I met and worked with, I did not feel passionate about it. I never felt like it was what I was meant to be doing. I saw it as a means to an end. I would often think, "The only way out is through", meaning that the only way out of our financial obligations to the society in which we live is to go through the steps. I saw my time in the car business as an out. I didn't really know there was another way to go, like following your passion. The truth is that there was always a nudge pulling me away from the car lot, but I lied to myself and ignored it.

When I finally left, my focus was to spend that time listening to my heart while I figured out what my next steps would be. I wanted to reconnect with the part of myself that was being forgotten. I wrote a lot, and eventually finished my third book, *Where Did the Gift Go?*. I didn't know exactly what I would do next or how I would do it; I just knew that writing and sharing it with others was a must.

Things got pretty tough over the years that followed. I went from having a good amount of disposable income to having almost no income. I used my savings and equity in assets to pay off the money I still owed to the previous owner of the car lot. I eventually went bankrupt, walked away from the home I owned, which was the place I lived for the longest out of anywhere, and sold most of my material possessions. At one time, my belongings consisted of a bed, nightstand, lamp, couch, table, books, two sets of sheets, a blanket, bookshelf, art, journals, pencils, pens, a laptop, a phone, a minimal amount of clothes, toiletries, surfboards, a skateboard, a bike, dishes (only a few), and a motor scooter. Although I have since acquired more things in excess of my needs, I still keep things to a minimum.

My life went from having an entire dealership of cars to drive at my disposal, to having a motor scooter as my main means of transportation. There is a lot that happened in between, but that is the very general gist.

As time passed, I ended up borrowing money from a dear friend to buy a car off of Craigslist. I found a 1987 Honda Accord for one thousand dollars. It had faded paint, and the air conditioner only worked half the time.It was a great car for what it was, but certainly a big step down from what I was accustomed to. Either way, I was grateful to have it at the time. The list of changes I made while repositioning myself to pursue my passion and dreams goes on, and by no means has been easy.

In this process, I began to ask myself questions about my core beliefs about money. Why did I feel like it was so important to leave something that I was passionate about (leaving my job working with youth for the car business), in order to have money? Why did

I think money would not only satisfy me and make me feel safe, but also fix me?

At one time, I was so driven to get it, but wasn't truly happy when I had it. Then, once I committed my life to following my passion and purpose, I struggled just to cover my basic needs. A big part of me didn't think I could follow my passion and still have money. I believed that it was one or the other, pursue your passion and be broke or do something you don't really love and have money.

When I left the car business, there was a part of me that believed I could and would make it on my own, but there was still the voice of my wounded child saying things to discourage and shame me. It was a back and forth in my own mind.

"You have to struggle if you are doing what you love."

"It's okay to not have money."

"You don't deserve to be happy."

"You can't have abundance and make a difference at the same time."

"You should have stayed in the car business."

Ultimately, the wounded child within was saying, "I don't know what real abundance looks like. I don't understand what happiness, sustainability, flexibility, freedom, contentment, travel, and wealth are. It feels foreign to me. Deep down, I am afraid of success. Since poverty is what I knew for so long, I would prefer to stay here. I am comfortable here."

The interesting thing about a poverty mindset that comes from childhood is that there is no difference between the belief that you have to work crazy hours, six days per week, at something that you are not passionate about, like I once was, and the belief that you have to be poor to do what you love. Both sides come from a place of limited belief in money and abundance.

As I went through many different phases of finding ways to sustain my visions and passions, I had to address what the wounded child within believes and works to convince me of on a regular basis. I know what I believe in my heart to be true, but my relationship with money and abundance can get clouded by the wounds of my past.

There are still times when I have to repeat mantras of abundance to myself. I write down that I am worthy of having abundance in all aspects of my life, including relationships and money, as a way of staying inspired. I know I deserve it, as we all do, regardless of what my wounded child, or yours, believes. I also know we don't have to be unhappy in order to have it.

I recommend that you have different affirmations about abundance that resonate with you and to repeat them often. I like writing down, "I am worthy of having abundance in all aspects of my life" because, to me, it is simple and inclusive. If this one does not work well for you, find one that does and write it down. Say it aloud as often as you need.

The more I have seen, and see, the root of my negative beliefs about money, the more I have been able to address them.

Take a few moments to reflect on your beliefs about money—and not just your belief, but where that belief comes from.

Abundance is not just about having money and buying things, either. It's about being happy, healthy, passionate, and fulfilled, while living a life you love. You could have millions of dollars, but, if you are not abundant in the other areas of your life, it doesn't really matter.

You don't have to grow up poor to have issues around money. Maybe you grew up rich, but the dynamics around it and the importance placed on having a lot of it cause just as much damage as not having it at all.

Perhaps you feel resentful toward money because you had a lot of it growing up, but still didn't get the love and attention you needed. In fact, you felt like your love and attention was bought, not given. Either way, there is no one issue that is worse than others. If you did have money, your wounds are no less worthy of attention than someone who grew up without a lot of it.

Work with your inner child's wounds as they relate to money and value. Honor the limiting beliefs, or other issues, you have because of them. Start the steps in creating a new way to see it. Encourage your worth. Facilitate your confidence in growing. Believe that, regardless of how much money there was, or wasn't, in your life at one time, you deserve to live a life of great abundance and joy. Not only do you deserve it, and deserve to be at peace with having it, but, by having the right thoughts, actions, and deep levels of trust, you will create an abundance of joy, health, friendships, opportunities, love, and money in your life.

Reflect and Engage

What were the finances like in your household when you were a child?

_____

_____

_____

_____

_____

_____

_____

_____

_____

_____

_____

_____

How do you think those experiences impacted your belief(s) about money now?

_____

_____

_____

_____

_____

_____

_____

_____

_____

_____

_____

_____

_____

_____

_____

_____

_____

_____

Were you ever told as a child that you couldn't have something because it cost too much? If you had money, were you ever told that you can have anything you want as an attempt to buy your love? Describe at least one experience you can remember.

_____

_____

_____

_____

_____

_____

_____

_____

_____

_____

_____

_____

_____

_____

_____

_____

_____

_____

How did it make you feel to be told you didn't have enough money? Or, if you had plenty, to feel like you were being manipulated by it?

_____

_____

_____

_____

_____

_____

_____

_____

_____

_____

_____

_____

_____

_____

_____

_____

_____

_____

Did you ever compare yourself to other kids based on what they had that you didn't, or what you had that they didn't? Did you feel lesser, or better, because of it?

_____

_____

_____

_____

_____

_____

_____

_____

_____

_____

_____

_____

_____

_____

_____

_____

_____

_____

_____

_____

Imagine yourself as a kid, wanting something specific on your birthday. Whatever that thing was, it was important to you at that time. Despite your conviction of wanting it, you were told, "No. We don't have enough money for that." On the other side of this, if there was plenty of money in your household growing up, imagine you really wanted your dad to be at your school play. He promised, "I will be there." As usual, he doesn't show. You get home, and there is a present on your bed with a note that says, "I'm sorry. I had to work late." See yourself as a kid, recalling the feelings of sadness, disappointment, and maybe even shame. Be present with the feelings that come up.

Now, imagine yourself walking up to you then, as a kid, and giving yourself that special thing that you really wanted but couldn't have because you didn't have enough money. Tell that inner child of yours not to worry about money—there is plenty to go around and you deserve having it. If you had money, imagine telling you then, as a kid, that you are so much more important than money and there is nothing wrong with having it, as long as you don't let it distract you from the things that matter most.

Side Note: I don't believe our young people should simply get whatever they want because they ask for it, and there are certainly times when there is just not enough money to get by. The example above is intended for illustration purposes to recall experiences that build into our limited mindset. On that note, there are always ways to tell young people "no", without fostering a negative belief about money. If they hear there is not enough over and over again, they will lose the ability to grasp anything different and always have the belief that "there is not enough". On the other hand, I understand that sometimes work or other commitments will take us from our family responsibilities. It is important to keep in mind that there is no replacement for being present, keeping your promises, and giving children the genuine love and attention they deserve.

You deserve all the best this life has to offer.

RELATIONSHIPS

C ommitted relationships connect us to what our inner truth about giving and receiving love is. The understanding we gained as a young person about love, and how it works, is a part of determining what issues come up for us, when we allow ourselves to become vulnerable to loving others and letting them love us.

It is necessary to be aware of what your issues are in order to cultivate healthy relationships. Work to understand how they may relate to the wounds of your inner child. The more aware you are of your issues, the better equipped you will be to deal with them.

As simple or silly as it may sound, keep a list of any

triggers you think may be attributed to your childhood. What you do with this list is up to you. You can try to identify the source of these triggers through journaling, meditation, and self-reflection. Write letters (that you may or may not send), like the ones we discussed earlier, to those who crushed your belief in love.

If you're comfortable doing so, it may even be helpful to discuss them with your significant other. While you're dealing with your wounded child, think about how your boyfriend or girlfriend must be feeling from the outside. If you are not currently in a relationship, talk with a close friend about any of your issues. Letting someone inside your mind can often help, both for your relationship and for you to sort out your feelings.

Although it is very helpful to have a loving, supportive, and understanding partner, no one else can heal your wounds but you.

Your partner can certainly help by being loving and supportive, but, ultimately, you have to manage the process. Understand, identify, and redirect the pain as it arises.

The tricky thing about healing wounds associated with love is that they don't generally come up, at least fully, when we are single. We tend to feel safe, secure, and untouched. When we do become involved deeply with someone, we are fine until we feel vulnerable. Eventually, we begin to have thoughts and feelings that were not there before. We now feel like we are in jeopardy of being hurt, so our fears, insecurities, and doubts slowly arise. We begin to act in ways that are not fitting to the person we worked so hard to become. Eventually, we stop being ourselves and become a reflection of the unhealed wounds of the child within. We begin to question everything our partner tells us, stalking their social media pages for reasons to believe they are cheating on us, getting suspicious when they get home late from work, or feeling anxious because they didn't call or text us back right away.

My old wounds have come up, in the past, more in some relationships than others, and I certainly didn't always have the most success at confronting them. However, I took, and still take, the need to address them seriously. Although I have fallen short on many occasions, I am happy to say that the work has paid off and I am in a great place with them. The moment I feel jealousy or a lack of trust brewing, I do my best to shut it down right away. Some impactful methods I've found include naming reasons why I am worthy, reminding myself that I will be okay no matter what happens, and simply closing my eyes and taking several deep breaths until the anxiety subsides a little bit. Regardless of what tools I use, I do my best to take hold of my mind—instantly. I say instantly because, the longer you wait to take control of the emotions being triggered and direct your mind in to a healthy place of being, the more disruption in your life they will cause.

When you feel the emotions of your wounds taking control, like you are losing your hold of them, remove yourself from the situation as soon as possible. There is nothing that you can say or do to react that will be productive in the heat of the moment. You need time to settle the emotions being triggered from your wounds. Take a walk. Go in the other room. Lie down. Tell yourself everything will be okay and that you don't need to fix it right now. Give it time and space. There is nothing that your significant other can say that will change what you feel in the moment, because, chances are, if you are already losing hold of your emotions, you aren't in the space to hear them anyway. I know this is much easier said than done, but I assure you that, the more you practice, the better you will get at it.

For so long I felt ashamed, discouraged, angry, and

broken in my relationships. I felt incapable of love. I started to believe that there was something wrong with me that would never be fixed. I would get so frustrated with how hard it was for me to love and be loved. On the other hand, I realized that these issues were deeper than simply not having the best experiences with love as a child. They were actually the wounds caused by those negative experiences that were never fully dealt with. This was a game changer of a realization for me.

On one level or another, we all doubt our worthiness of love, whether it is consciously or unconsciously. Am I good enough? Can I trust this person? What if they leave or cheat on me? Why don't they love me like I love them? I am unworthy of their love... so on and so on.

Does this mean you are doomed to not have a healthy relationship? No. It simply means you need to be more aware and willing to address the issues as they come up. Communicate with your partner. Be kind to yourself, as well as to them, when their wounds are triggered.

Wounds associated with love are no different from other wounds. They need love, care, and attention for them to heal. Granted, you can get through life without acknowledging them or putting any time or energy into healing them, but your relationships, and life in general, will be much better when you do.

You deserve to know just how special you are, and to experience wholesome, loving, supportive, healthy relationships. The wounded child within you deserves it. I deserve it. We all deserve it.

Reflect and Engage

Describe what love was like for you as a child.

_____

_____

_____

_____

_____

_____

_____

_____

_____

_____

_____

_____

Growing up, was your family affectionate with one another? Loving? Supportive? Encouraging? Nurturing? Explain.

_____

_____

_____

_____

_____

_____

_____

_____

_____

_____

_____

_____

_____

_____

_____

_____

_____

_____

_____

_____

When is the first time you remember having your trust broken by someone you loved? Describe the experience. How did it make you feel then, and how does it make you feel now to think about it?

_____

_____

_____

_____

_____

_____

_____

_____

_____

_____

_____

_____

_____

_____

_____

_____

_____

_____

_____

Can you identify at least one issue you had, or currently have, in your relationship(s) that you think may be related to your childhood? What is something you can do to address it (them)?

_____

_____

_____

_____

_____

_____

_____

_____

_____

_____

_____

_____

_____

_____

_____

_____

_____

_____

_____

Read this aloud to yourself:

The more I continue to address the wounds that cause problems in my relationships, the more freely I will be able to love and be loved.

I deserve to be loved, fully and completely, always.

BE EASY ON YOURSELF

There is a part, sometimes just a small part, of most of us that feels like we are never enough, because we never felt like enough as a child. By being hypercritical of ourselves, we feed into the wounds of the child within.

Think about all of the times you've doubted yourself because of others' negativity. How many times in your childhood were you discouraged from doing something because other people didn't believe you were capable? How about the times when you were told you weren't good enough, made fun of, or called hurtful names? What about the times when you needed to be lifted up, but instead people put you down?

Other people—be it teachers, parents, relatives, siblings, friends, or peers—have created your self-doubt. The negativity of others in your childhood facilitated your feelings of not being enough then and potentially cause you not to feel enough now.

As we get older, those wounds play out over and over again. We talk to ourselves terribly. We criticize every mistake we make. We avoid trying new and exciting things because we believe that we are not good enough. What if I fail? What if they don't like me? What if I look silly?

That mindset was created from past wounds. It's not your fault.

When the negative self-talk starts, be easy on yourself, and, above all, don't believe it.

You don't ever deserve to be talked down to, called hurtful names, or told you are not enough, especially from yourself.

Be nice to yourself. You have insecurities that are not because of you, but from the hurtful words and action of others. The self-doubt you may have, and the need to be so critical to yourself, stem from something beyond your control.

Remind yourself, often, that you are enough. In fact,

you are not just enough; you are more than enough. You are worthy and capable of doing anything and everything you desire in your life.

If those were the messages that were continuously given to you as a child, you would not have to contend with the negative self-talk you endure now. Even when people are brought up in a loving and supportive environment, the world can still be very hurtful.

Where your wounds come from is not as important as seeing the need to heal them.

You have the power to heal your wounds and free yourself from the discomfort they cause in your life.

It takes a lot of work. It isn't as simple as waving a wand, saying a chant, or meditating for it all to go away. There is no quick fix. Unfortunately, it is a lifelong process. Even when you feel mostly healed from childhood wounds, there are still wounds that have developed between then and now, and ones that will surface in the future. Whatever the case, the process is not an easy one, but it is so worth it.

Pain will surface. It's okay. Be kind to yourself, and be patient. Keep working to address the wounds that cause you to be so hard on yourself in the first place by changing your self-talk. Pay attention to the narratives that play in your head. Are you continuously putting yourself down, doubting your self, or being hypercritical about everything you do? If you are, try creating a different story in your mind—one that will build you up instead of breaking you down. Cultivate positive self-talk by feeding your mind with positivity. Read inspirational books, watch uplifting talks, listen to encouraging podcasts, and spend time with positive people. Build your self-esteem by doing things that are good for your mental, physical, and spiritual health. When your mind, body, and spirit are in good health, you will be better prepared to refine the way you talk to yourself.

Reflect and Engage

On average, how many times per day do you think you put yourself down? Give at least one example of how you put yourself down at some point this week.

_____

_____

_____

_____

_____

_____

_____

_____

_____

_____

_____

Give an example of a recent time when you were hypercritical of yourself.

_____

_____

_____

_____

_____

_____

_____

_____

_____

_____

_____

_____

_____

_____

_____

_____

_____

_____

_____

As a child, what did your parent(s) or guardian(s) do when you made a mistake? Broke something? Got a bad grade on a report card?

_____

_____

_____

_____

_____

_____

_____

_____

_____

_____

_____

_____

_____

_____

_____

_____

_____

_____

_____

How often were you complimented or given words
of encouragement and support when you were a kid?
How did you feel about it?

_____

_____

_____

_____

_____

_____

_____

_____

_____

_____

_____

_____

_____

_____

_____

_____

_____

_____

What is something people would call you as a young person (a name, a trait) that you are still self-conscious about now?

_____

_____

_____

_____

_____

_____

_____

_____

_____

_____

_____

_____

_____

_____

_____

_____

_____

_____

_____

Write down a list of things you wish you heard more as a young person. How do you think it would have impacted your life?

_____

_____

_____

_____

_____

_____

_____

_____

_____

_____

_____

_____

_____

_____

_____

_____

_____

_____

_____

Spend at least one minute writing down positive things about yourself. Let the compliments and encouraging words flow.

<u>I am</u>:

_____

_____

_____

_____

_____

_____

_____

_____

_____

_____

_____

_____

_____

_____

_____

_____

_____

_____

HEALING THE CHILD

The thought of healing your inner child may seem strange. It may even feel overwhelming to consider. To think about your actions, reactions, emotional outbursts, negative thoughts, and/or hurtful behavior coming from the wounds from your past is not easy. However, if they are not healed properly, they will continue to manifest into your life over and over again.

We often separate ourselves from the wounds we experienced as a child, as if they are no longer a part of us. There seems to be a general misconception that they will magically go away on their own as we get older. Just because we have learned to incorporate them into our life, and even let them go to some extent, does not mean we have healed them.

When you speak positively to yourself in the midst of the wounds of your inner child being triggered, you teach him or her something new. The hurting side of your inner child (the part of you that has unresolved wounds) then feels loved, supported, and nurtured, which will organically foster healing the wounds around the trigger. The wounded child within will begin to feel safe. Beyond treating yourself well in the midst of emotional triggers, it is important that you also do so on a regular basis.

Be nice to yourself, always. Celebrate your accomplishments, regularly. Commend your efforts to be who you are, often.

When you do things to celebrate your accomplishments, you are not only acknowledging your present self, but you are also acknowledging the child within you that may have never felt supported or loved. Every good thing you do for yourself in the present also fosters the sense of worthiness in the part of you from the past that doesn't feel that way.

For some of us, the only recognition we did get as a child was bad. There was no acknowledgement of the good we did. We were only acknowledged for what we did wrong. On top of that, we were mistreated and hurt because of others not having a hold on their own issues. Their own pain manifested into the distorted ways they hurt us. This is where fear of making mistakes and taking risks comes from. Over time, the pain mounts and chips away at your well-being. Eventually, you stop being the real you, the you that is relentless, fearless, confident, and resilient.

When you peel back the layers, it's not your fear as an adult holding you back, so much as it is your wounds from childhood.

Every time you make a mistake, say something positive to yourself. Be reassuring, encouraging, supportive, motivating. Build yourself up! No matter how many mistakes you make, or don't make, you're still amazing. You're still worthy. Beyond that, be nice to yourself in general, not just when you make a mistake or have a victory. You deserve to be treated nicely, especially by yourself.

I know how difficult this can be. I get unbelievably hard on myself when I make mistakes. In fact, I'm hard on myself in general, mistake or no mistake. It is just something I do, and I continuously work hard to change that. I know a lot of it stems from the wounds caused by being ridiculed and called hurtful names as a child, feeling invisible.

You wouldn't believe how quickly it can play out for us to be hard on ourselves. I was driving down the road after leaving my house when I realized I forgot a notebook I needed for a meeting later in the day. I would not have time to get it later, and I was already running behind. Going back to get the notebook did not help. When I realized I forgot it, I instantly called myself stupid. "Ah…. You are so stupid. Why would you do that?"

Being talked to like that may feel normal to the wounded child within, but, for me as an adult, not so much. Speaking to myself that way is not acceptable. We would not appreciate being spoken to that way by someone else, so why do we accept it from ourselves?

I had to correct myself and reassure the child within that is afraid of making mistakes and doesn't feel good enough that it's okay to mess up sometimes. I switched my self-talk to be more positive, and focused on things I did right up to that point in my day. I felt better instantly. I wasn't stressed. I knew everything would be okay. The best part is, I didn't spend the next several hours condemning myself and reinforcing the wounds that made me call myself stupid in the first place. I have gotten caught in downward spirals like that in the past, as I'm sure we all have.

Calling myself stupid was a default reaction based on the way I was programmed to acknowledge and handle my mistakes. This is just one of many examples I can use. It is not just about being hard on ourselves when we make mistakes; it is about the way we feel deep down about who we are, and how the wounds from our childhood are connected to that.

The wounds may all look different on the surface, but they are very much the same beneath it. Regardless of what the wounds are, how they play out in your life, or what examples I give of them, at the root, there is some level of pain, lack of self-worth, guilt, shame, resentment, or anger. The way to effectively heal them is to address them with love, patience, and understanding.

If you change the way you treat yourself, and look at some of your "issues" as wounds to be healed, not things that hold you back, you will create an unparalleled sense of freedom in your life. When you do the work to heal the wounds of your inner child, you will live your life with greater peace and fulfillment.

One of the greatest ways to heal the wounds caused by the mistreatment of others is to remember, and stay true to, who you are. Regardless of what happened in your past, or may even be happening now in the present, don't be held down because you are hesitant to deal with it. Do the work to heal your wounds, and the rewards will be plentiful.

Reflect and Engage

What is at least one recurring issue in your life? What feelings and/or painful memories do you think are at the root of it?

_____

_____

_____

_____

_____

_____

_____

_____

_____

_____

_____

What does the wounded child within you need to hear and/or experience on a regular basis in order to be healed? What do you need to hear more of, in general?

_____

_____

_____

_____

_____

_____

_____

_____

_____

_____

_____

_____

_____

_____

_____

_____

_____

_____

_____

How do you currently address yourself when you make mistakes? How about when you are stressed or anxious about something?

_____

_____

_____

_____

_____

_____

_____

_____

_____

_____

_____

_____

_____

_____

_____

_____

_____

_____

_____

_____

What are at least three things you can do to facilitate a better sense of love and belonging for the wounded child within?

_____

_____

_____

_____

_____

_____

_____

_____

_____

_____

_____

_____

_____

_____

_____

_____

_____

_____

_____

You Have the Power to Choose

You cannot always control what challenges you face, just like you cannot control what your childhood was like. However, no matter what you do or do not experience, you have the power to choose how you will respond to these challenges and if you will allow them to control your life.

You choose to rise or fall.

I understand that the range of abuse, struggle, and obstacles that any of us may face, or has faced, is different. Beyond my own personal experience, I have heard countless inspiring stories of people choosing to redirect their life no matter how hard things were. I am certain you have this same power.

Ultimately, the best way I have come to understand the power we all have to choose whether we rise or fall is through my own efforts to not be controlled by the wounds from my childhood. Often times, those wounds manifested themselves into violence, anger, rage, and a general sense of disregard for my life. I felt like I was fighting just to be seen, heard, and loved. I was falling to my wounds, circumstances, and the issues caused by them, not rising above them.

When I was lying in the hospital bed with nine holes in my body from the street fight I mentioned earlier, I was not just in the process of falling to my anger. I fell to it, and, because of that, I almost died.

Being stabbed that many times, as bad as it was, awakened me to the fragility of life, and the gift it truly is to be alive. After that night, I slowly started to believe in my own value and worth as a person. When I got out of the hospital, all of my anger was still there. I still got into fights, felt angry at the world, and had no clue how to fix myself. I found solace in writing and eventually separated myself from people and situations that were not healthy. I became acutely aware of my triggers with anger and the need for the once-raging child within me to act out. At first, I would completely avoid anything that triggered me, even in the slightest. I didn't trust myself to manage my anger.

The first time I knew I'd finally healed that part of my wounds was about five or six years after the stabbing. I was out with a friend, and he got into an argument with a guy as we were walking into a club. Things quickly became heated between them, and they got in each other's face. When I tried to separate them, the person my friend was arguing with took a swing at my face and grazed my left cheek. Everyone watching, including my friend, expected to see a fight. I looked at him, feeling very confident in my ability to hurt him easily, as I'd been training for a boxing tournament I had later that month. Instead, I stared into his eyes, smirked, and walked away. My friend couldn't believe it, and, quite honestly, neither could I. Seeing the work I was doing to heal myself pay off was inspiring. I felt more powerful in that moment than I ever had beating someone up. I rose above the pain, anger, rage, and resentment, and, as cheesy at it sounds, it made all the difference in the world.

I chose, and still choose, to become someone different from who the wounds from my past would have led me to become if I'd let them. I have risen, and will continue to rise, above challenges and adversities, instead of being held back and down by them. I have faith that you can do the same.

This is not to say that all of my wounds have gone away entirely. They just don't control my life anymore.

I chose to become a survivor, a warrior, instead of staying stuck as a victim. I now use the wounds of my childhood as part of my motivation to inspire others to overcome their own challenges.

Everything you do in, and with, your life is a choice. No matter how hard you once had it, or how much you let self-doubt control you, or how afraid you may get, or how discouraged you are, you have the power to choose how you will respond and who you will become.

Connect with the truth inside of you that knows you deserve the best. Embrace the resilience of the human spirit that has driven people to do amazing things with their lives, despite when the odds were against them.

No matter how strong or courageous we may be, by nature, it takes our choosing to harness that strength and courage to make a difference. It is our responsibility to keep rising above the things that will hold us back if we let them, including the negative experiences from childhood.

Every experience gives you the opportunity to learn, grow, and, in some way or another, help others, if you choose to do so. Choose not to be held back by your circumstances or wounds. Once you make that choice, keep rising above them day in and day out. You have already risen so high, and above so much. Keep rising!

Reflect and Engage

Who do you choose to become from the adversities you have faced, or will face, in your life?

_____

_____

_____

_____

_____

_____

_____

_____

_____

_____

_____

How can you use what you have learned from your own experiences to help others?

_____

_____

_____

_____

_____

_____

_____

_____

_____

_____

_____

_____

_____

_____

_____

_____

_____

_____

_____

What is one specific challenge that you faced as a young person, during which you rose above?

_____

_____

_____

_____

_____

_____

_____

_____

_____

_____

_____

_____

_____

_____

_____

_____

_____

_____

_____

_____

How does it make you feel when you overcome challenges in your life? Have you honored yourself for all the ones you have?

_____

_____

_____

_____

_____

_____

_____

_____

_____

_____

_____

_____

_____

_____

_____

_____

_____

_____

_____

SEE YOUR VALUE

At some point in our childhood, we all experienced something that compromised the perception of our self-worth. For some of us, it was quickly healed by an abundance of love and support that surrounded us. For others, we continued to experience things that reinforced the feeling of not being valued. Every time I was hit, called a hurtful name, or not paid much attention to at all, I felt less and less valued, until eventually it was clear to me that I wasn't.

When we don't see the value in who we are, it manifests in various ways. From suicide, to staying in unhealthy relationships, to having no ambition, to poor health, to drug abuse, lack of self-worth can be at the root of many problems. When I no longer saw the value in who I was, it became really hard for me to see the value in others. In the midst of the pain I caused and the things I did to get attention, what I ultimately wanted was to feel like I was important, special, and that my life meant something. I wanted to feel valued.

A child with low self-worth eventually becomes an adult. We then carry the hurt and shame of never feeling good enough as a child into our daily lives as adults. Our wounds are masked with one distraction after another.

Intellectually, as adults, we can read self-help books, recite positive affirmations, practice self-love, and even pray or meditate in order to find peace and feel better about our life. All of these are very important, and great to incorporate into your life, but, until you identify and address the root cause of your struggle with self-worth, you will never truly be free.

The core beliefs that you have about yourself began a long time ago. They are anchored deep in your mind, replaying the same messages over and over again, messages like, "You are not good enough," "No one will love you," and "You are a failure."

Reflect on your wounds.

Think about the times you first experienced not feeling loved and appreciated.

Can you feel the pain of the innocent child you once were?

Has anyone ever told that hurting child how important he/she is? How amazing they are? How great they are? Have you told that wounded child of yours how much he or she is valued?

Sit with your emotions. Get to the root of any thoughts you have that no longer serve a purpose to your existence. Affirm how special you are and know that you were just as important then, as a child, as you are now.

Your worth should never be questioned.

Although you may not have had any control over who hurt you, or who didn't, in your past, you do have control over seeing your worth now, and not accepting anything but the level of love and respect you deserve.

Your self-worth may have been compromised by the poor choices of others, and/or the painful experiences you had in the past, but there is no person or experience that can ever change the truth in who you are. Your job is to not only believe those words and imbed them into your consciousness, but also to convince the wounded child within to believe how amazing he/she is, despite how many times they may have been made to believe otherwise. There are many things you can do to create a consciousness of valuing yourself and others, as well as convincing the child within to do the same:

- Practice self-love every day
- Help others
- Set firm boundaries on how you will be treated and stick by them
- Feed your mind with positive content (affirmations, books, podcasts, etc.)
- Spend quiet time via reflection or meditation
- Make time to be in nature

Most of all, live your life in a way that brings you joy, a sense of purpose, and fulfillment.

Reflect and Engage

What does it mean to you to feel valued?

_____

_____

_____

_____

_____

_____

_____

_____

_____

_____

_____

_____

How often did you feel valued as a child? Most days? Every day? Rarely? Never? Elaborate as much as you see fit.

_____

_____

_____

_____

_____

_____

_____

_____

_____

_____

_____

_____

_____

_____

_____

_____

_____

_____

_____

_____

Name at least three things that make you feel valued
as an adult.

_____

_____

_____

_____

_____

_____

_____

_____

_____

_____

_____

_____

_____

_____

_____

_____

_____

_____

Please read the paragraph below aloud, to yourself, as many times as you need. In fact, if you feel inspired to do so, write it down and read it every morning for however long you see fit.

Just because others may not have always made me feel valued as a child doesn't mean that I wasn't. I am deserving of the very best this life has to offer and will not accept any treatment that is less than what I deserve. I see the value in who I was as a child, as well as who I am as an adult. I will continue to value my inner child in times of weakness and believe in the amazing person I am, always.

I (*insert your name*) am valued.

Conclusion

I hope everything I've shared with you in this book has provided a great deal of value for you. Nothing I've shared is meant to minimize your views, perceptions, or ideals about how things of our past influence, or don't influence, our present. The intent is to give you a fresh look at things that may be holding you back, and inspire you to address them in ways that will help you live a healthy, happy, and full life. There is no absolute in any of this. Take to heart the parts that really resonated with you, and forget about the rest. Going inward and facing past pains is not easy. In fact, it can be downright scary and discouraging, so be proud of yourself for taking these courageous steps.

Most importantly, keep seeing the greatness in who you are and doing the things that build you up and best facilitate your growth and healing as an individual.